BUDAPEST

THE CITY AT A GLANCE

CW00381602

Four Seasons Hotel Gresham P...

This sumptuously restored art n...
Secessionist former insurance c...
complete with Zsolnay ceramics...
glass from Miksa Róth, opened as...
2003 and once again became a city landmark.
See p030

Design Terminal

The communist-era Erzsébet tér bus station is
proof that not everything associated with that
regime is bad. István Nyíri's 1949 Corbusian
Volánbusz building was a glimmer of optimistic
design, before the shutters of socialist realist
architecture came clanging down from above.
It now houses a contemporary design centre.
Erzsébet tér

Modern and Breitner building

Since it was completed in 1912, the front of the
Jugendstil-like former department store has
been a meeting place for Budapesti couples.
See p012

Chain Bridge

Based on a design for London's Hammersmith
Bridge, the first permanent link between Buda
and Pest opened in 1849 and led to growth and
modernisation. Its Scottish engineer, Adam
Clark, became a minor national hero.

The Palace of Arts

Gábor Zoboki's impressive cultural complex
boasts the acoustically outstanding Béla Bartók
National Concert Hall and the beautifully
lit Ludwig Museum of Contemporary Arts.
See p076

Castle District

Come here to stroll down cobbled streets
among UNESCO-protected medieval buildings,
and for the city's best view.

INTRODUCTION
THE CHANGING FACE OF THE URBAN SCENE

Hungary's lovely capital wears its history on its sleeve. Whether it be grand, belle époque hotels or communist-era coffee shops full of wizened smokers playing dominoes, the past never seems too far away. The political divisions between right and left that coloured so much of Budapest's 20th century continue to be played out, sometimes in museums of torture and statue parks, and sometimes on the streets, as the riots of 2006 demonstrated.

Yet while the past lingers, there is a distinct whiff of the future in the air. Hungary's EU membership means investment is starting to flow, the country's entrepreneurs have had 15 years to get used to consumer capitalism and confidence is on the up. Barely a month goes past without a high-style restaurant opening its doors, as the Budapesti reassert their love of eating and drinking, and dazzling hotels are being carved out of fabulous art nouveau buildings.

After junking everything from the communist period, as the city rushed to embrace Western goodies, Budapest has hit a new era, where designs and brands from the past have been reinvented, partly as ironic retro chic and partly as a statement of renewed national pride. Meanwhile, in the decaying buildings of the old Jewish ghetto, where renovation rattles on at a pace, the arty 'ruin pubs' and the rash of underground fashion boutiques point to a Budapest that is finally finding its own way of dealing with the modern age. Go now and catch a city on the cusp.

ESSENTIAL INFO

FACTS, FIGURES AND USEFUL ADDRESSES

TOURIST OFFICE
Budapest Tourism Office
Március 15th tér 7
T 322 4098
www.budapestinfo.hu/en

TRANSPORT
Car hire
Sixt
Könyves Kálmán körút 5
T 451 4220
www.sixt.hu
Metro
T 461 6688
www.bkv.hu/metro
Taxis
City Taxi
T 211 1111
Fo Taxi
T 222 2222

EMERGENCY SERVICES
Ambulance
T 104
Fire
T 105
Police
T 107
24-hour pharmacy
Teréz Gyógyszertár
Teréz körút 41
T 311 4439

EMBASSIES
British Embassy
Harmincad utca 6
T 266 2888
www.britishembassy.hu
US Embassy
Szabadság tér 12
T 475 4164
budapest.usembassy.gov

MONEY
American Express
Deák Ferenc utca 10
T 235 4330
travel.americanexpress.com

POSTAL SERVICES
Post Office
Petőfi Sándor utca 13-15
T 318 3947
Shipping
UPS
Airport Business Park
Lőrinci utca 61
T 877 0000

BOOKS
The Book of Fathers by Miklós Vámos
(Abacus)
Under the Frog by Tibor Fischer (Vintage)
Fatelessness by Imre Kertész (Vintage)

WEBSITES
Architecture/Design
www.octogon.hu
Newspaper
www.budapestsun.com
Magazine
www.pestiside.hu

COST OF LIVING
**Taxi from Ferihegy Airport
to city centre**
£11.50
Cappuccino
£1
Packet of cigarettes
£1.20
Daily newspaper
£1.40
Bottle of champagne
£27

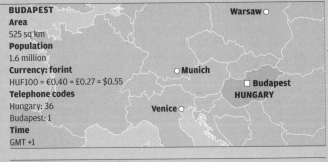

BUDAPEST
Area
525 sq km
Population
1.6 million
Currency: forint
HUF100 = €0.40 = £0.27 = $0.55
Telephone codes
Hungary: 36
Budapest: 1
Time
GMT +1

Warsaw ○

○ Munich

□ **Budapest**
HUNGARY

Venice ○

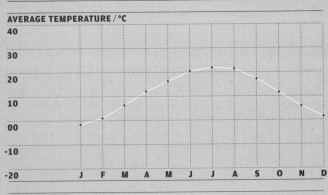

AVERAGE TEMPERATURE / °C

40											
30											
20											
10											
00											
-10											
-20	J	F	M	A	M	J	J	A	S	O	N	D

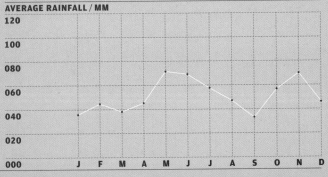

AVERAGE RAINFALL / MM

120											
100											
080											
060											
040											
020											
000	J	F	M	A	M	J	J	A	S	O	N	D

NEIGHBOURHOODS

THE AREAS YOU NEED TO KNOW AND WHY

To help you navigate the city, we've chosen the most interesting districts (see below and the map inside the back cover) and colour-coded our featured venues, according to their location; those venues that are outside these areas are not coloured.

FERENCVÁROS

Not long ago, Ferencváros was notable only for being the city's working-class district and the home of Hungary's biggest football team. But recent years have seen a spate of developments spinning out from the pedestrianised thoroughfare Ráday utca, with its endless row of bars and boutiques. In the summer, nightclubs open up in buildings and empty spaces along the riverside road Közraktár utca.

TERÉZVÁROS

Stroll along leafy Andrássy út to browse the new designer furniture shops, the A4 Apple Center (Andrássy út 4, T 453 3939), the wi-fi cafés and of-the-moment restaurants, and Budapest will come across as a fully paid-up, 21st-century member of the EU. Keep going past Oktogon metro station and the House of Terror (see p034) to remind yourself of how much has changed before sampling the café culture of the city's gorgeous young things in Liszt Ferenc tér.

ERZSÉBETVÁROS

The border between Districts VI and VII runs down Király utca, a renovated strip of chic restaurants and contemporary design centres. The rest of District VII continues to gentrify and conservation groups are springing up to defend its unique boho character. It remains the centre of Eastern Europe's largest Jewish community. Look for the 'ruin pubs' in its back alleys and some interesting shops selling old tat.

MARGITSZIGET

For decades, the Budapesti have gone to bathe, exercise, cycle and meet their lovers on green, tear-shaped 'Margaret Island'. It can be accessed from the river crossings, Margit and Árpád, that touch its northern and southern tips. In the summer it buzzes with open-air drinking venues and hosts a music festival, while year-round you can swim in its pools (see p069 and p092) or book a treatment at its spa (see p094).

LIPÓTVÁROS AND BELVÁROS

The downtown heart of Pest is chock-a-block with neoclassical, eclectic and art nouveau piles from the city's belle époque, particularly in the business district of Lipótváros. There is tourist tat on the Váci utca, running down the middle of Belváros, and historic cafés, pleasant squares and posh hotels aplenty. Sas utca and Zrínyi utca, which intersect in front of St Stephen's Basilica (Szt István tér), are dotted with the city's most stylish restaurants.

VÁRHEGY, VÍZIVÁROS AND TABÁN

The walled Castle District, Várhegy (see p037), is a UNESCO site with imposing palaces, baroque streets, Gothic churches, underground labyrinths and stupendous views. Below is the emerging riverside area of Víziváros, where contemporary design is on show in shops and stylish hotels. To the south, Tabán boasts the Rudas Bath (see p089), and Gellért is home to the eponymous spa (see p089).

LANDMARKS
THE SHAPE OF THE CITY SKYLINE

The geological rift that brings the Danube to Budapest explains why one side of the river rises steeply into the hills of Buda and the other is as flat as a billiard table. Looking from Pest, this means the skyline is dominated by the buildings on the high ground on the other side of the river. Buda has two major elements: to the north, the Castle District (see p037), with its looming Royal Palace; and to the south, the Gellért hill, which is dominated by the Liberation Monument and the Citadella. The landmark featured in Buda, the Moszkva tér metro station (see p014), doesn't so much shape the skyline as shape the daily lives of thousands of Budapesti. Similarly, in Pest, the Modern and Breitner building (see p012) is a social landmark because of its continued use as a meeting place, despite the demise of its department store.

Other sites we could have chosen include the Chain Bridge, which opened in 1849, and the Gresham Palace (see p038), once owned by a British insurance company and now a Four Seasons hotel (see p030), which the bridge meets on the Pest side. But instead, we've picked buildings with the kind of architectural and social history that makes them talking points for the city, including Erick van Egeraat's much debated ING building (see p010). Also, look out for the communist-era bus station, now reinvented as a contemporary Design Terminal (Erzsébet tér).

For full addresses, see Resources.

ING building
Erick van Egeraat's jaggedly energetic office building is loved by some, dismissed as theatre by others, and ignored by no one. The sloping structure is divided into three distinct edifices, connected by two glass-fronted asymmetrical atria. The main elements are clad in folded and creased strips of glass, aluminium and stone and suspended on a concrete frame.
Dózsa György út 84b

Modern and Breitner building

Formerly a department store and now
an unremarkable collection of shops,
the Modern and Breitner building has
remained a true city landmark, thanks to
its position near the entrance to the Deák
Ferenc tér metro station. Here, all three
of the underground lines intersect, making
the building a traditional meeting place
for generations of Budapesti. It was built
between 1910 and 1912 and designed by
Sámuel Révész and József Kollár in high
German Jugendstil style, with graceful
sculptural mouldings that emphasise
its vertical lines and underlying frame.
The corner was once topped by a cupola,
and its removal means the building's
upward thrust now appears somewhat
truncated. After WWII, it became a store
specialising in East German goods. With
a neat symmetry, today it carries a large
permanent sign for Audi cars.
Deák Ferenc utca 11-13

Moszkva tér metro station
What a joy it must have been to see
this building in its socialist heyday,
before fast-food signage disrupted its
expressionistic message of dynamic
progress towards the workers' utopia.
István Czeglédi's 1972 design still copes
splendidly with hordes of travellers
as they stream under the overhanging
fan of the skyward-shooting roof.
Moszkva tér, www.bkv.hu

HOTELS

WHERE TO STAY AND WHICH ROOMS TO BOOK

You almost get the impression that most Budapesti were employed as stonemasons during its 'Golden Age', from 1867 to WWI – it would seem the only explanation for how an entire city of imposing neoclassical, eclectic and art nouveau buildings was constructed in so short a time. There are streets and streets of them, giving plenty of scope to developers looking for properties to turn into a new generation of five-star hotels.

The best looking, best located and simply the best is the Four Seasons Hotel Gresham Palace (see p030), which since its £70m restoration in 2003 has joined the list of Europe's most fabulous hotels. Other major hotels in restored buildings include the huge Corinthia Grand Hotel Royal (Erzsébet körút 43-49, T 479 4000) and the teetering-on-the-edge-of-ludicrousness Boscolo New York Palace (see p025), where the all-white atrium appears to have been constructed using the plans from a particularly outré wedding cake. Others are still waiting for restoration. The Danubius Hotel Gellért (Szent Gellért tér 1, T 889 5500), connected to one of the city's great spas, is undergoing a facelift.

New builds are also getting a look-in. The neat and quirky Art'otel (see p026) on the Buda side of the Danube was the first to open, but up the road from here near the Chain Bridge a new designer hotel, as yet unnamed, broadens the options.

For full addresses and room rates, see Resources.

Parlament

This is a nicely designed four-star hotel in the downtown business district for those whose travel budget runs to the chic and cheerful. It opened in 2006 and provides a setting and amenities to a fairly high standard for its price, although the rooms, such as the Standard Double (above), aren't so big that you'd want to bring lots of pals back. The glass-roofed breakfast room (overleaf) is elegantly modern and the jacuzzi, while not a patch on some of the city's luxury spas, makes for a relaxing, arty bolthole. The 'happy hour' free tea, coffee and pastries in the late afternoon and free internet access add up to a pretty good package. There's no restaurant, but it's just a minute's walk to the cluster of classy eateries around St Stephen's Basilica. *Kálmán Imre utca 19, T 374 6000, www.bestwestern.com*

Breakfast room, Parlament

Andrássy Hotel

As well as being a perfectly good four-star boutique hotel in embassy row, the Andrássy allows you to stay in a building designed by one of Hungary's undoubted architectural and, bizarrely, sporting heroes. Alfréd Hajós was the country's first ever Olympic swimming champion, winning at Athens in 1896 while still an architecture student. He went on to design the stunning swimming pool on Margitsziget (see p092) and, in 1937, this Bauhaus building, now a hotel. The Andrássy has some stylish and graceful public spaces, including the acclaimed Zebrano restaurant and terrace. Rooms are small in comparison with the lobby areas (above), but are very comfortable despite being a touch plastic-fantastic. *Andrássy út 111, T 462 2100, www.andrassyhotel.com*

Le Meridien

A former insurance building on one of Pest's main squares, this hotel has an interesting, or dubious, history as the city's police HQ from 1948 until 1997. The current mayor of Budapest spent time in its cells and it played a key role in the 1956 uprising, when police chief Sándor Kopácsi refused to order his men to fire on protesters and then agreed to the toppling of the building's red star. The renovation in 2000, by Tibor Kolbe of Mérték Építészet Stúdió, has produced a superior-style chain hotel. The grand lobby is topped by a glass atrium, overlooked by an elegant fourth-floor terrace (above). Rooms, such as the Deluxe (overleaf), have French windows, Persian rugs and high ceilings.
Erzsébet tér 9-10, T 429 5500,
www.lemeridien.com

Deluxe Room, Le Meridien

New York Palace

Where the Gresham Palace (see p030) restoration is an exercise in high-quality decorum, the Italian Boscolo group has taken another old insurance building and shown all the restraint of Liberace's dresser. The colonnaded floors rising above the lobby-atrium (left) are up-lit to emphasise their wedding-cake whiteness, the Italian furnishings are camper than a West Hollywood flower-arranging class and the rooms rustle with the sound of heavy silk. Glamour has been piled on by the bucketload; yet it makes us smile. The Royal Suites are made out with blue (above) or red colour schemes, but the standard suites are a more manageable sage, gold and brown. The hotel is connected to the uproarious New York Café (see p056). *Erzsébet körút 9-11, T 886 6111, www.newyorkpalace.hu*

Art'otel

Each hotel in this chain started by the German developer and collector Dirk Gädeke features interiors worked on by one artist. Here it's the American painter and printmaker Donald Sultan, famous for his large, brightly coloured still lifes. There are works hung throughout the hotel, in the Chelsea Restaurant (above) and the other public areas, and hundreds of prints and drawings in the halls and guest rooms, each of which also includes a black cast aluminium bird by Sultan. Carpets, as in the Superior Room (right), elements of the interior design and a fountain were also designed in collaboration with the artist. The building sits by the river on the Buda side and has a pared-down modern frontage of stone and glass, while the back has incorporated a sympathetically restored row of old fisherman's houses.
Bem rakpart 16-19, T 487 9487, www.artotel.hu

Kempinski Hotel Corvinus

The Kempinski chain is linked to Lufthansa and Germany is Hungary's number one tourist source, so it's no surprise that this was one of the first international brands to open here post-communism. Rooms, such as the master bedroom in the Presidential Suite (above), are luxuriously appointed, and the setting, next door to Le Meridien (see p021) on Erzsébet tér, is perfect for the fashion district of Deák Ferenc utca. Hungarian designers Jozséf Finta and Antal Puhl gave it a soaring lobby that became a central meeting point for the city's emerging élite. Having been around since 1992, it was for a long time the best bed in town for the likes of Madonna and Helmut Kohl. The competition is tougher now, and the group had to splash out on major renovations, such as the Kempinski Spa and Cactus Garden (right), to keep up. *Erzsébet tér 7-8, T 429 3777, www.kempinski-budapest.com*

Four Seasons Hotel Gresham Palace
Originally designed by Zsigmond Quittner
and completed in 1906, the Gresham
Palace offers a sublime hotel experience.
The combination of riverside location
(ask for a room with a view of the bridge
and Buda), high-style Secessionist
setting, as seen in the lobby (pictured),
and impeccable service is unsurpassed.
Roosevelt tér 5-6, T 268 6000,
www.fourseasons.com

24 HOURS

SEE THE BEST OF THE CITY IN JUST ONE DAY

Central Budapest is fairly compact, so travelling around presents few problems; indeed you can walk between most places on our itinerary. If you do want a taxi, order one rather than hailing them on the street, which can lead to irritating negotiations. A better bet is the three-line metro system, which is pleasantly simple to use. The yellow underground route was the first to be built in Continental Europe, using a cut-and-cover method; in places it is only a few feet below the road, and at some stations you can see the street up one flight of stairs while sitting on the train. The only place where the lines intersect is at Deák Ferenc tér.

The tree-lined and bustling artery of Andrássy út makes a good jumping-off point. Start by having breakfast just off it at Mai Manó (opposite). From here it is a 10-minute walk to the memorial to victims of the 20th-century's totalitarian ideologies at the House of Terror (see p034). For lunch, the best located branch of Leroy Café (see p036) is the one on Ráday utca, a pedestrianised street that is lined with cafés and fascinating shops.

Spend the afternoon across the river in hilly Várhegy, Buda's Castle District (see p037), before crossing back to Pest for drinks at Gresham Palace (see p038). Round your day off on the Danube with a floating dinner in the sleek, modern interior of the moored boat Spoon Café & Lounge (see p060).

For full addresses, see Resources.

10.00 Mai Manó Café

Eschewing the gilded coffee pleasure palaces of the 19th century, which are full of tourists and usually overpriced, an insider's tip for a morning cup of java and a light nibble is the little café nestling at the bottom of the Hungarian House of Photography. It's a youngish, arty hangout popular with the fashion mag folk and offers a long list of coffees and pastries. In the summer, sit outside and watch Budapest amble past. Mai Manó was Hungary's leading photographer until his death in 1917; the eight-floor museum, which is worth a look in its own right, was his studio and family home.
Nagymező utca 20, T 473 2666, www.maimano.hu

11.00 House of Terror

This neo-Renaissance mansion was used as a torture centre by Hungarian fascists and later by communist Soviets. Designer Attila F Kovács was hired in 2002 to turn it into a museum to the crimes of the 'Double Occupation', and his stark 'Terror' stencil juts out from the roof. It is a compelling counterpoint to Statue Park (see p100). Andrássy út 60, T 374 2600, www.terrorhaza.hu

13.00 Leroy Café

Part of the Tamás Sztanó and György Lefkovics empire, there are seven Leroy cafés dotted round Budapest, including a fairly formal one in the shadow of St Stephen's Basilica. But on a summer's day, sitting outside the Leroy on the café/bar strip of Ráday utca off Kálvin tér, you can feel part of the new and confident Budapest. The menu offers well-executed Asian-tinged fusion standards, a light version of Hungarian cuisine and sushi. There are a number of interesting shops nearby, such as Ráday Galeria (T 217 6321), which is fitted out in deco-style black and chrome, and sells ceramics, jewellery and sculpture.

Ráday utca 11-13, T 219 5451, www.leroy.hu

15.00 Castle District

With most of the action taking place on the Pest side of the river, it can be easy to miss out on the historic Castle District that looms over the city. The best way to take in the view and get to the area is to cross the Chain Bridge, constructed by Scottish engineer Adam Clark in 1849, and take the funicular railway that crawls up the hill. Cars require a permit inside the UNESCO-protected quarter, so the Gothic streets are eerily quiet. Visit the Hungarian National Gallery (T 204 397 325) and the Budapest History Museum (T 224 3700) in the Buda Palace. Or amble along enjoying the otherworldly ambience and the view over Pest from the white cloisters of the Fishermen's Bastion (above).

20:00 Gresham Palace

If you're not actually staying at the Four Seasons Hotel Gresham Palace (see p030), go for cocktails to take in the splendid ground-floor lobby. Zsolnay tiles cover the walls, Miksa Róth's mosaics have been restored, the peacock gates are stunning and the glass cupola ceiling is the icing on the cake. *Roosevelt tér 5-6, T 268 6000, www.fourseasons.com*

URBAN LIFE
CAFÉS, RESTAURANTS, BARS AND NIGHTCLUBS

Budapest's going-out culture has seen so much change in recent years that there has been a blurring of the difference between a café, a bar and a restaurant. Whatever a venue calls itself, most options have improved, and Liszt Ferenc tér and the area around the Basilica witness the opening of stylish destinations every other week. Restaurant cuisine and décor have taken leaps forward, with lighter versions of traditional fare being served up in retro-styled commie canteens such as Menza (overleaf) and screamingly hip haunts like Dió Restaurant & Bar (see p044). Cocktail joints have proliferated, from the Gresham Palace (see p030) to Negro (see p055).

Meanwhile, many of the gilded *kávéház*, one-time hangouts for doomed revolutionaries and soon-to-be exiled actors, have been refurbished, such as Gerbeaud (Vörösmarty tér 7, T 429 9020) and the New York Café (see p056), while others, like the Danubius Hotel Astoria (Kossuth Lajos utca 19-21, T 889 6000), continue to supply coffee and cakes in lush (albeit slightly faded) surroundings. Many of the changes to Budapest's bars and restaurants have been moves in an international direction, but the city is also holding on to its own indigenous socialising culture, nowhere more so than in the 'ruin pubs', such as Szimpla Kert (see p046) and West-Balkán (Kisfaludy utca 36, T 371 1807), which have been built into the courtyards and rooms of abandoned buildings.

For full addresses, see Resources.

Tranzit Art Café

A little out of the city centre, the Tranzit Art Café is worth the trip for the building alone. Originally a small, beautiful bus station built in 1965 by Félix Vilmos, it was converted into a restaurant in 2005 by the Budapest architects MCXVI, who left the delightful winged roof and double-height glass walls alone. In summer, the eating area extends out to under the inverted canopies that once provided shelter to those waiting for a bus. The menu is basic, well-executed café fare – breakfasts, soups, salads and sandwiches – and a programme of art exhibitions, discussions and music attracts an interesting and lively clientele.
Kosztolányi Dezső tér, T 209 3070, www.tranzitartcafe.hu

Menza

The contemporary Hungarian cuisine on offer at Menza is sumptuously well done, plus you get to eat it in an ironic reworking of communist chic. Designer Istvan Muszai has produced a fairly faithful take on a 1960s canteen – a riot of orange and brown, leatherette couches and so-bad-they're-good lamps.
Liszt Ferenc tér 2, T 413 1482,
www.menza.co.hu

Dió Restaurant & Bar

Budapest restaurant design either plumps for an international, contemporary look or a commie-retro feel. István Muzsai, who chose the latter for Menza (see p042), has gone a third way at the relatively new Dió. Here he chose to blend contemporary styling with traditional ceramic-tile motifs and carved walnut panels. Executive chef István Szür opts for the same approach, adapting classic Magyar ingredients to modern gastronomy. Think deer *filet mignon* with fried quail's eggs and truffle ravioli or wild boar tenderloin with dried strawberry sauce. Although part-owned by television presenter András Sváby, Dió attracts more than just the media crowd, and the serving staff thankfully don't suffer from ideas above their station. *Sas utca 4, T 328 0360, www.diorestaurant.com*

Tom George

Named after its owners – Budapest's restaurant empire-builders Tamás Sztanó and György Lefkovics – Tom George makes an unashamed bid for the wallets and eyes of those who like their restaurant to be as trendy as their outfit, although the clientele don't actually wear pink shag-pile carpets, unlike some of the walls. Lefkovics constantly travels, looking for restaurant-design ideas to bring home, and there's certainly little on the menu to tell you that you are in Hungary, with the exception of a few Magyar fusion elements. Otherwise Tom George offers mostly east Asian dishes and has a highly regarded sushi bar, which is saying something in a landlocked country. In summer, the action moves outdoors, where there is a view up the street to the Basilica.
Október 6 utca 8, T 266 3525

Szimpla Kert

Romkocsma, or 'ruin pubs', have now taken over some of Budapest's many abandoned buildings. But Szimpla is more than just a pub – it hosts film clubs, bike-repair tutorials, exhibitions, bands and DJs. Although it is entered through what looks like a squatter's bedroom, it attracts a friendly, mixed-age crowd. *Kazinczy utca 14, T 352 4198, www.szimpla.hu*

Gundel

This has been a Budapest institution since 1910, when Károly Gundel took it over and started the Frenchification of Hungarian cuisine with the creation of its legendary pancakes. It was acquired by George Lang and Ronald Lauder in 1991, and rescued from the torpor of its communist decades with an expensive refurbishment that retained the best of its art nouveau décor, including a work by Hungary's most famous 19th-century artist, Mihály Munkácsy. Chef Kálmán Kalla prepares light versions of national specialities served (for a clientele that is tourist-heavy in the summer) on Zsolnay china, from the factory that made the tiles for the Gresham Palace (see p030). *Állatkerti utca 2, T 468 4040, www.gundel.hu*

Merlin

Prized by the *beau monde* of Budapest for its electric atmosphere, this art deco substation has been transformed by the Hungarian design agency Lipsip into a cosmopolitan club, restaurant and theatre space. The gallery-level resto-bar retains an industrial feel, with prominent ducts and whitewashed walls onto which films, and the bar menu, are projected. Down the spiral stairs is a performance space that has played host to both puppet shows and the Royal Shakespeare Company, as well as its own English-language theatre company. Of late, Merlin has also become Budapest's venue of choice for parties, fashion events and concerts – anything from indie and electro to funk and hip hop, drawing a young and stylish crowd.
Gerlóczy utca 4, T 317 9338, www.merlinbudapest.org

Goa

This restaurant, with its great Andrássy location, gives the eateries around St Stephen's Basilica a run for their money. Opened by Frigyes Novák and his wife, Kriszta Késmárki, who are also owners of an ethnic interior-design store, Goa has a minimal but warm décor, featuring flagged floors, unadorned walls and chunky wooden tables. The cuisine on offer is Asian fusion and was influenced by former executive chef James McClure's 10 years working in the Far East. McClure's signature dish, the spice-encrusted 'black and blue' tuna, is still on the menu and a regular order. Other treats include the Malaysian duck salad and the sushi menu. *Andrássy út 8, T 302 2570, www.goaworld.hu*

Mokka

A recent makeover has toned down this Moroccan-tinged French restaurant's more clichéd ethnic elements – the décor is now a combination of backlit art boxes, Maghreb lamps and leather furnishings. Highlights from chef Rezső Boksay's menu include swordfish tartare in lime-grenadine jelly on a mixed salad.
Sas utca 4, T 328 0081,
www.mokkarestaurant.hu

Dokk

This is a stage for preening yourself on. The music is less important than your look, your access to the VIP area and the size of the SUV you pulled up in. If Szimpla (see p046), a non-profit outfit, is one version of post-communist culture, Dokk is capitalism run rampant, wearing wannabe Manolos and a fake tan. The club, which is situated inside an old shipbuilding warehouse, even includes a couple of tiered stands on either side of the dancefloor, to allow you to see and be seen. It is located on an island in the Danube (take a taxi from downtown) and has a terrace bistro, although the food will be even less the point than the music. The *New York Post* called it a 'meat market', so don't say you weren't warned. *Hajógyári sziget 122, T 0630 535 2747, www.dokkdisco.hu*

Negro

Once you get over its ill-judged name, Negro is the place to see the rich, the young and the beautiful enjoying some of the best cocktail-mixing talent the city has to offer. Before Negro, a Budapest cocktail was flat tonic and a gin with a label containing two spelling mistakes. After it opened in 2004, with a look created by interior designer Attila F Kovács, the rest of the city's bars started producing cocktail menus – but only the bar at the Four Seasons Hotel Gresham Palace (see p030) really offers serious competition. The location, in the square in front of the Basilica, is an astounding backdrop during the summer; make a reservation if you want a table outside.
Szent István tér 11, T 302 0391

New York Café

In the same building as the New York
Palace hotel (see p024), this café is an
authentic Budapest legend. It was a
hangout for Alexander Korda, Michael
Curtiz, Peter Lorre and Bela Lugosi pre-
WWI, when they worked in the nascent
Hungarian film industry. Its restoration,
by designer Adam Tihany, reflects the
high style of the main hotel and the café's
original features – all excessive gilding,
moulding, ornate lamps, statuary,
ceiling paintings and a white baby grand.
Then, not altogether jarringly, there
are plain modern furnishings with mirror-
topped tables and low-rise poufs, and
chill-out music. Groups of actors do short
plays, in Hungarian, between the tables
from time to time, so don't be alarmed.
Erzsébet körút 9-11, T 886 6111,
www.newyorkpalace.hu

A38

The A38 was a hulking great Ukrainian stone carrier transported to the Danube and remodelled by László Váncza, the Hungarian architect who is working with Zaha Hadid on a stunning new office development for Szervita Square in downtown Pest. A38 comprises a concert venue and nightclub space in the hold, a restaurant in the contemporary space of the glassed-in deck (above) and a terrace for the summer, with other rooms, such as a VIP bar (overleaf), dotted around the place. The complex attracts people from the creative industries, but the age range varies depending on the night. Tickets for gigs can be bought online. *Buda side of Petöfi Bridge, T 464 3940, www.a38.hu*

VIP bar, A38

Spoon Café & Lounge

While not as externally striking as the other permanently moored boat on the Danube, A38 (see p057), Spoon has a sleek modern interior that contains two restaurants, five bars and a chilled-out 'oriental' lounge. Make reservations in the classy café for fine dining; semicircular banquettes in the middle of the room make for a particularly cosy atmosphere if you are in a group. Executive chef Beke Zsolt has produced a menu of progressive and innovative fusion dishes – St Jacob's mussels grilled with honey-flavoured pomegranate nectar, for example, and Thai risotto. Afterwards, chill on the terrace or get with the groove in the lounge.
Pier 3, Vigadó tér, T 411 0933, www.spooncafe.hu

INSIDER'S GUIDE
ZSUZSA KÁRPÁTI, MAGAZINE EDITOR

Zsuzsa Kárpáti is editor of the Hungarian style magazine *Pep!* and lives in Ferencváros. Her hectic schedule means she rarely eats proper, home-cooked food, so when she does manage to get away from her computer, she plumps for a traditional vegetable dish called *főzelék* at the Főzelékfaló (Hercegprímás utca, T 266 3193); after the first spoonful she feels as if she's at her mother's. Like all good Budapesti, Zsuzsa loves pastries, and believes the best in town are at Daubner Cukrászda (Szépvölgyi utca 50, T 335 2253). Its *pogácsa* filled with cheese is, she says, 'godlike', but be prepared to queue for a long time. For dinner, she favours Menza (see p042) for its 'great retro style'. Its name may evoke a communist-era canteen, but the food is bang up to date.

In the evenings, if going pubbing with friends, her favourite meeting place is Szimpla (see p046), a cool hangout that is always full, although she suggests that (like most underground places) the bottled beer is better than the draught. For clubbing, she picks and chooses according to the gig: After Music Club (Nyár utca 6, T 0620 551 5111) has an indie night every Friday, and once a month Hungarian indie bands perform at Trafó Bár Tangó (Liliom utca 41, T 215 1600). For fashion shopping, Zsuzsa recommends Retrock Deluxe (see p087), where some of the more creative Hungarian labels can be found, including Je Suis Belle and Nanushka.

For full addresses, see Resources.

ARCHITOUR

A GUIDE TO BUDAPEST'S ICONIC BUILDINGS

Budapest provides lots of opportunities on the architour front. A number of its civic buildings, including Ödön Lechner's ground-breaking former Postal Savings Bank (see p070) and Béla Lajta's New Theatre (opposite) are not only highly individual, but also important because they predicted the coming of art nouveau and art deco respectively. The city also provides visitors with the opportunity to study how the twists and turns of the 20th century's dominating ideologies have impacted on the supposedly apolitical act of putting up buildings.

The former Postal Savings Bank is one such case – constructed to encapsulate feelings of swelling Hungarian nationalism, but then proving too eccentric for a reactionary government that insisted on a return to eclecticism. Similarly, the Palatinus Lido (see p069) and former Ministry of Transport and Postal Services (see p067) are examples of monumental architecture stuffed with modernist and classicist ideas, so beloved of dictators in the 1930s. Elsewhere, it is the dictatorship of the people that defined styles in the postwar period, whether in clean-lined, optimistic builds such as the former Trade Union Headquarters (see p078) or in the importance attached to designing transport hubs for the masses at Moszkva tér metro station (see p014) and the Erzsébet tér bus station (see p009), now a design centre.

For full addresses, see Resources.

New Theatre

This is an absolute delight of a building, which on completion as the Parisiana nightclub in 1909 was more than 10 years ahead of its time in deploying elements that would become associated with art deco. It was designed by Béla Lajta, a student of Ödön Lechner, the father of the 'Magyaros' movement. Lajta's building included stepped, ziggurat-like doorways, which architecture critic Edwin Heathcote sees as alluding to the entrance of a tomb: nightclub as underworld. A frieze of dark angels supports the blue lettering of the Parisiana sign. The building, which was first converted into a theatre in 1919, was altered after both World Wars. In the late 1980s, it was restored, using the original designs, by Tamás König and Péter Wagner. *Paulay Ede utca 35, T 269 6021, www.ujszinhaz.hu*

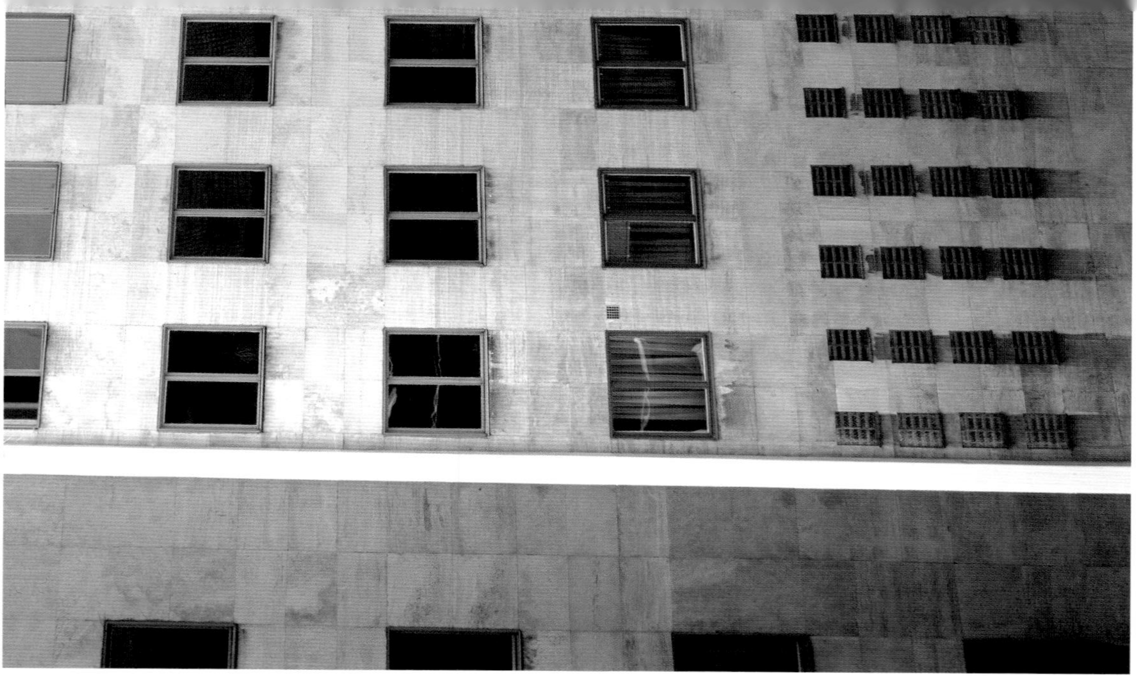

Ministry of Transport and Postal Services
Masses of blank-faced marble spread over
an enormous building, statues of national
heroes, and use as a ministerial building:
one imagines that the dictator Horthy had
spent some of the prewar years visiting
Mussolini's Italy. And yet there is something
about this former Posta building located
in Erzsébetváros that defies the heavy-
handed monumentalism of 1930s dictator-
tecture. The presence of a second, lower
elevation drags the building back to
something like the scale of its neighbours,
and the wraparound horizontal bay adds
a certain amount of dynamism to the
whole thing. Gábor Boda's eight statues
of the original tribal elders of the Magyars
also work less as heroic nonsense and
more as deco-ish detailing, if writ large.
Dob utca 47

Transformer Station

This building really sorts out the brutalist men from the boys, taking no prisoners in a way that will leave many of modernism's fellow travellers behind. It is basically a very big brick, housing equipment only. And although its scale is in keeping with the buildings that surround it, that's the only thing that is. They feature ornate detailing, while the Transformer Station laughs in the face of decoration; they adhere to the city's grid pattern, while the Transformer does its level best to disturb it. Designed by architect Ernő Lestyán in 1969, this is one for purists. *Dob utca 10*

Palatinus Lido

The lido is another prewar public building that has elements of fascist modernist classicism about it. The simple loggia with its bare columns and flat roof could grace any number of Italian structures of the same period designed for leisure. Margitsziget island has several pools, including one designed by the country's first swimming champion (see p092) and there are health spas dotted around its verdant lanes. But István Janáky's 1937 lido building makes the Palatinus the most interesting architecturally.
Margitsziget, T 340 4505

Former Postal Savings Bank

Ödön Lechner's triumph and singular
contribution to central European
architecture is this former Postal Savings
Bank. As the instigator of the Magyaros
school, Lechner is linked to Jugendstil
and the Secessionists, but the sheer
exuberance of the curves and colours of
this building's glazed brick façade and
roof line and his use of Hungarian folk
motifs and designs make it a highly
individual precursor to modernism in its
own right. In designing it at the turn of the
19th and 20th centuries and by escaping
Continental historicism and eclecticism,
Lechner predates Otto Wagner in Vienna.
The nationalism inherent in the design
and the materials – the glazed bricks and
tiles were from the Zsolnay ceramics
factory – was also an important element,
for this was to be a new kind of bank to
be used by small savers all over the country.
Hold utca 4

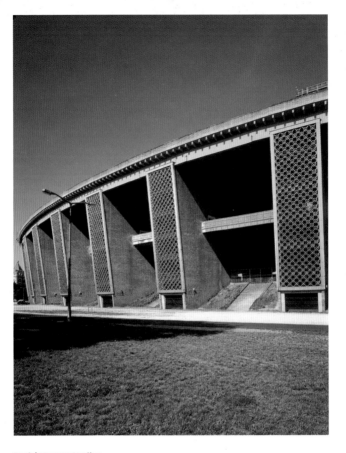

Puskás Ferenc Stadion

Previously known as the Népstadion (People's Stadium) until 2001, when it was renamed after Hungary's most famous footballing son, this is the place where England suffered their worst ever defeat, losing 7-1 to Hungary in 1954, which should make it a must for visiting Scotsmen. It was built in proper socialist style – that is in relatively short order between 1950 and 1953, thanks to the help of massed 'volunteers'. The design is an oval style by Károly Dávid with great, cantilevered concrete floodlights leaning in over the crowds and huge flights of steps to allow departure en masse. As ever with quickfire Stalinist structures there are problems with the detailing and finish, but it remains an impressive presence, even if Hungarian football no longer lives up to the setting. *Istvánmezei út 3-5, T 471 4100*

Nyugati Station
Gustave Eiffel turned the iron and glass structure of the roof into the centrepiece of this station, completed in 1877, and so created one of the gems of European railway architecture and engineering. The glass front also means that the trains become part of the building and streetscape. A commuter station has been added sympathetically.
Nyugati tér, T 392 3800

The Palace of Arts

Even Gábor Zoboki, the architect of this cultural centre, which opened in 2005, admits the ear was more important than the eye in the design of the concert hall. Together with the world's best acoustician, the octogenarian Russell Johnson, Zoboki strove to create a hall that was acoustically rich and isolated from outside noise. Their solution was to isolate the Béla Bartók National Concert Hall inside a floating box sitting on a rubber and steel bed. It has been hailed by both critics and musicians as a rival to Russell Johnson's other acoustic masterpiece, the Symphony Hall in Birmingham. Also housed in The Palace of Arts is the smaller Festival Theatre concert space and the Ludwig Museum of Contemporary Arts (left). The main concert hall attracts the world's best orchestras; ask your concierge about tickets.
Komor Marcell utca 1, T 555 3001, www.mupa.hu

Former Trade Union Headquarters
Despite what some say was a bland 2002
refurbishment by Erick van Egeraat, the
1949 TU building, a simple pre-Stalinist
lightbox of glass and reinforced concrete
in the leafy embassy district, remains
one of the most important modernist
buildings in the city. Owned by the ING
bank, it now contains offices, including
those of Egeraat's firm, EEA.
Dózsa György út 84a

SHOPPING

THE BEST RETAIL THERAPY AND WHAT TO BUY

In retail terms, Budapest is perched on the verge of an explosion. In the first phase of post-communism, mass market brands moved in, shopping malls went up and art folk set out their stalls on the Váci utca in the heart of the downtown tourist trail.

After years of patchy economic growth, Hungary's accession to the EU in 2004 is set to bring a new phase of development and investment. More goods catering to the luxury sector are on their way and already shops are being refitted so that Gucci et al can join the advance guard of Louis Vuitton. However, the country is small, with a population of 10 million, so the space for a significant high-end contemporary sector, selling Hungarian-designed fashion, furniture and accessories is limited, despite the fact that new stores open enthusiastically on Andrássy út all the time.

For this guide, we've picked out the best of Hungarian design available now and also looked to the past a little, tracking down some unique mid-century pieces, political memorabilia and some interesting gewgaws that you won't be able to find anywhere else. Cutting-edge clothes designers unusually gather under one roof at Retrock Deluxe (see p087), while Geppetto (opposite) is a showcase for contemporary furniture design. And it's still possible to find Bauhaus and Jugendstil bargains in Budapest, as canny Western dealers know, at Studio Agram (see p085).

For full addresses, see Resources.

Geppetto

Hungary's small contemporary furniture and accessory design sector has thrown up some real talent in Márton and Máté Elek. The brothers started designing and manufacturing by hand for friends and relatives in 1996. As demand grew, they concentrated on interior, object and furniture design, outsourced production, and were the first Hungarians to exhibit at 100% Design in London and at the Salone Satellite in Milan. They work with clients on one-off pieces, and sell signature items, such as the 'ASK' rocking chair, from £405, in their store-cum-gallery (above). Another jewel is 'AIR1', from £4,050, a pair of sleek, electrostatic loudspeakers produced in association with the sound engineer Zoltán Bay.
Katona József utca 15, T 270 0107, www.geppetto.hu

Nosztalgia

This is the place to come for that large oil painting of Lenin looking into the middle distance that you've always wanted. Nosztalgia has plenty, also a few of Marx and lots and lots of busts of the pair of them, made from every conceivable material. There's even one of Uncle Joe Stalin lurking on a shelf, although it's hard to imagine he's a great draw for even the most irony-laden treasure hunter.

György Máj's ramshackle shop, just off the main drag of Rákóczi utca, also has a nice line in old Hungarian Communist Party lapel badges, interwar Hungarian movie posters, teddy bears, radios the size of sideboards, old camera equipment and enough treats among the battered old tat to keep you happily browsing for quite some time.

Klauzál utca 1, T 322 8848

Zwack Unicum

Hungary's national drink, sold in a black bottle shaped like an anarchist's bomb, gets its name from the Habsburg Emperor Josef II, whose royal physician, Dr Zwack, concocted it for him as an aid to digestion. *'Das ist ein Unikum* [one-off],' the Emperor was said to say in 1790, on sampling this alcoholic concoction of 40 herbs. And well he might, as it tastes like a particularly bitter cough syrup and has a strength that is as likely to cause as many health problems as it could possibly cure. It is sold everywhere, but visit the Zwack museum to make sure you get a bottle at source. It will likely remain one of those drinks that you only get out very late at night. But it has an emergency cross on the bottle, so it must be good for you. *Soroksári út 26, T 476 2383, www.zwack.hu*

Studio Agram

At the end of a street lined with shops dripping in gilt-framed oil paintings, dandy porcelain, swords and all sorts of ornate baubles, Studio Agram is a blast of refreshing modernism. It specialises in furniture and objects from Jugendstil and art deco right through to the 1970s. Co-owner Zeljko Kvarda has contacts in Italy, Romania, the former Yugoslavia and Ukraine as well as Hungary, bringing him interesting pieces that he often repairs and recovers before putting on display in his eminently browsable two-floor store. Despite the mini-boom in communist-retro gripping Budapest, 85 per cent of Studio Agram's sales still go to foreigners, often dealers looking for Eastern bargains. The shop can also advise on shipping overseas.
Falk Miksa utca 10, T 428 0653
www.studioagram.com

Tisza Cipö

Once all of Hungary wore Tisza Cipö shoes; they had no choice. The company started off making army boots and eventually was making 10 million shoes a year (not bad, considering Hungary's population was, er, 10 million). Its cheap plastic trainers were an attempt to prove that communist fare could compete with smuggled Adidas. (It couldn't.) Tisza trainers disappeared for a decade, but the brand has since been brought back to life by entrepreneur Vidák László. The 'T' logo has survived, and there is an element of 1970s styling in the new shoes and sportswear, but the quality is a million miles better. In a neat twist, Tisza Cipö are now on sale in the West. *Károly körút 1, T 266 3055, www.tiszacipo.hu*

Retrock Deluxe

Many of Hungary's best and most creative fashion designers do better overseas than they do at home, where tastes remain conservative. The place to see them all is the neat little two-floor boutique Retrock Deluxe, not to be confused with its sister store Retrock (T 0630 678 8430), which sells more grungy and often second-hand gear. The Deluxe store carries lines from the trio behind Use, whose minimalist black designs are selling well in Japan; from Szandra Sándor's Nanushka range, now exporting to LA; some of Auh Tuan's intricate handmade leatherwear; and occasional items from the pair of fashion consultants behind label Je Suis Belle. Women's is upstairs, men's is downstairs, and beware – they don't take credit cards.
Henszlmann Imre utca 1, T 0630 556 2814, www.retrock.com/deluxe.htm

SPORTS AND SPAS

WORK OUT, CHILL OUT OR JUST WATCH

Budapest is located above a deep geological fault line. The rift draws the Danube into a channel, and from this fissure, 1,000m below the surface, come the 130 thermal springs that feed the city's spas with their heat and minerals. There is no metropolis quite like it and, unsurprisingly, water features a great deal in the city's leisure activities, whether it be for healing purposes or simply for swimming in. Don't leave Budapest without experiencing at least one of its excellent spas (opposite and see p094).

Hungary's gift to the football world was Gustav Sebes' Golden Team of the early 1950s, which included the marvellous Ferenc Puskás. They almost won the World Cup and humiliated England. The squad was broken up by the 1956 uprising and, despite fielding a few good sides in the 1960s and 1980s, Hungarian football has been in long-term decline. Ferencváros, the country's biggest club, was removed from the top division in July 2006 for failing to meet the financial requirements of the league, and its fans are notorious for their racist and anti-Semitic chanting.

Hungary's other great sporting talent is fencing, and Budapest's best fencing school is at the Honvéd (see p090). There is even a fencing style named after the country, and Hungary ranks second only to France in the all-time Olympic medal table for the sport, a remarkable achievement given the size of the population.
For full addresses, see Resources.

Rudas Bath

There have been healing spas in Budapest since the Romans were here. For sheer luxury, the recently reopened spa in the bowels of the Corinthia Grand Hotel Royal (see p016) is best, while the neoclassical splendour of the main swimming pool at Gellért Bath (T 466 6166) is probably the city's most famous, although it is in dire need of some sprucing up. Even older is the Turkish-built hammam Rudas, on the Buda side, which locals will tell you is *the* spa hangout since a refurbishment in 2005. The 16th-century building features a three-storey, classically colonnaded main pool, six smaller pools (above), an Ottoman cupola, three saunas and two steam rooms. *Döbrentei tér 9, T 356 1322, www.spasbudapest.com*

Honvéd Fencing Club

Housed in a former synagogue, designed in 1908 by the Hungarian temple builder Lipot Baumhorn, who studied with Ödön Lechner, this club trained Bela Imregi, before he fled Hungary in 1956 and went on to coach generations of champion British fencers. Contact the Hungarian Fencing Federation (T 252 2149), rather than just turning up, foil in hand. *Dózsa György utca 55*

Alfréd Hajós Sports Swimming Pool
In 1896, architecture student Alfréd Hajós
was Hungary's first Olympic gold medallist.
He went on to become the country's top
designer of swimming pools, although he
did also design some hotels (see p020).
The triumph of his Bauhaus pool is the
concrete four-storey platform for the high
diving boards. The modernist rectangle
makes a fine backdrop for morning laps.
Margitsziget, T 340 4946

Danubius Health Spa Resort

The drab Soviet-era hotel attached to this spa was designed by Kéri Gyula in 1979 and refurbished in 2000, but its modern, medicinal and high-tech spa is a must for those who are really serious about the healing properties of all sorts of minerals. It's a veritable balneotherapeutic behemoth.
Margitsziget, T 889 4700, www.danubiushotels.com

ESCAPES

WHERE TO GO IF YOU WANT TO LEAVE TOWN

Hungary, thanks to the Treaty of Trianon in 1920, which divided up the spoils of the former Austro-Hungarian empire, is only about one-third of the size that it used to be. This means that if you travel in any direction out of Budapest for a few hours, you'll most likely find yourself in another country.

Our escapes don't quite require you to go that far, but you might want to consider an overnight stay if you take a trip to Eger (opposite), partly because of its distance from Budapest, and partly because one of the best reasons to go there is to get pleasantly sozzled in the surrounding first-class wineries. The Hotel Senator-Ház (Dobó-Platz 11, T 36 320 466) and Hotel Korona (Tündérpart 5, T 36 313 670) are probably the best in town.

Requiring less effort on your part is a trip up the Danube to some of the historic towns of the Danube Bend, such as Esztergom and Visegrád (see p102). Rather than an attempt to tick off more baroque buildings, this should be seen as an excursion in which the getting there is most of the point. If your time is limited, it would be a shame to visit Budapest and miss the unique delights of the socialist monuments gathered at Statue Park (see p100) on the outskirts of the city. No longer having the power to oppress means Marx, Engels, Lenin and their Hungarian counterparts have a chance to impress on a more aesthetic level.

For full addresses, see Resources.

Eger

About 130km north of Budapest, Eger is an extremely pleasant historic town, the site of an Ottoman siege in 1552, set amid the gentle Bükk Hills. The downtown has been called the Baroque Pearl of Europe and is worthy of a film location. Once you have had your fill of castles, churches and the like, head a short way out of town for what makes Eger really worth visiting: Szépasszonyvölgy, which translates as the Valley of Beautiful Women and is the centre of local wine production. There are dozens of small wineries selling cheap and good quality plonk out of dark cellars. This is where to find the famous Egri Bikavér (Bull's Blood), Hungary's dry red blend of Eger wines. Those with a non-Hungarian palate might want to avoid Médoc Noir, a rich sweet red. Before you set out from Eger, book a taxi to pick you up afterwards.

Esztergom

About 60km north of Budapest, charming
Esztergom isn't just a place, it's something
of a state of mind, especially if you are a
Hungarian nationalist (you can also arrive
by a trip up the Danube, see p102). It was
home to the first Magyar kings and was the
capital of Hungary from the 10th to 13th
centuries, seeing off a couple of Mongol
invasion attempts in the 13th century, only
to fall into ruin under the Ottomans as
Buda prospered. It's still the headquarters
of the Hungarian Catholic Church, hence
the massive, neoclassical 19th-century
Basilica on Castle Hill (right). The Basilica
is also the resting place of the trenchantly
anti-communist Cardinal Mindszenty,
who died in exile, but whose posthumous
homecoming in 1991 has made it a place
of pilgrimage for Hungarian right-wingers.
Climb the narrow steps to the top of the
cupola for stupendous views – that's
Slovakia on the other side of the river.

Statue Park
Budapest's graveyard for its communist statuary is a windswept yard around 45 minutes by taxi from Pest. Expect to find the startling memorial to Béla Kun, leader of the brief 1919 Hungarian Soviet republic, by Imre Varga, and all the usual May Day suspects. Where else can you go these days to see a statue of Lenin hailing a taxi?
Balatoni út/Szabadkai utca, T 424 7500,
www.szoborpark.hu

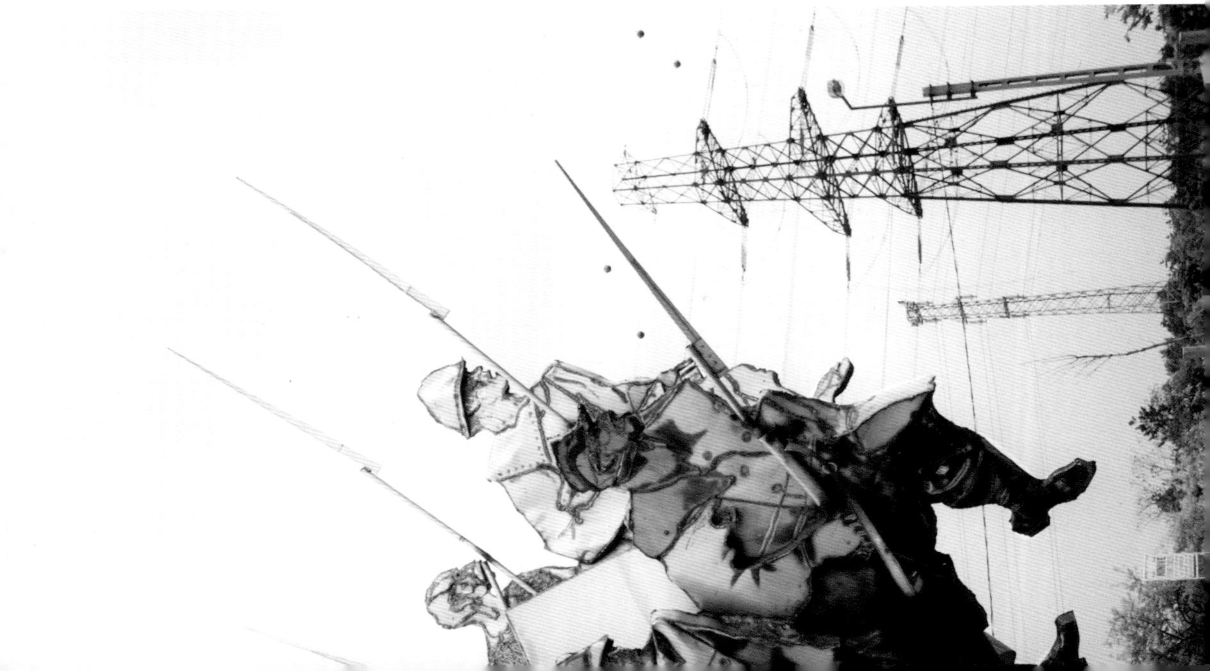

Visegrád

Around 40km north of Budapest, the Danube makes a 90-degree lurch to the south. This stretch of river between the bend and the city is a pretty valley and can be enjoyed by taking a leisurely boat trip to the historic fortress town of Visegrád. Its 13th-century citadel, once a repository for the Hungarian crown jewels, announces your arrival as it looms into view high above the river.

NOTES
SKETCHES AND MEMOS

1. Maimano (p. 033)
2. Menza (p. 042)
3. Szimpla Kert (p. 048)

Easy Hotel - 132€   £66 ea.
Teréz város

Mandragora - 168€   3 Nights
£84. each

~~Extra Club~~ - £247

Kerbs - Peobrade
Merlin
A38.

- A38 - Barabás love   WED

  Jazz, trumpets,
  500ft   9pm, roof terrace

- Merlin

- Pesticide.

RESOURCES
CITY GUIDE DIRECTORY

A

A38 057
 Buda side of Petöfi Bridge
 T 464 3940
 www.a38.hu
After Music Club 062
 Nyár utca 6
 T 0620 551 5111
 www.aftermusicclub.hu
Alfréd Hajós Swimming Pool 092
 Margitsziget
 T 340 4946

B

Budapest History Museum 037
 East Wing
 Buda Palace
 Szent György tér 2
 T 224 3700

D

Danubius Health Spa Resort 094
 Margitsziget
 T 889 4700
 www.danubiushotels.com
Danubius Hotel Astoria 040
 Kossuth Lajos utca 19-21
 T 889 6000
 www.danubiushotels.com/astoria
Daubner Cukrászda 062
 Szépvölgyi utca 50
 T 335 2253
Design Terminal 009
 Erzsébet tér
Dió Restaurant & Bar 044
 Sas utca 4
 T 328 0360
 www.diorestaurant.com

Dokk 054
 Hajógyári sziget 122
 T 0630 535 2747
 www.dokkdisco.hu

F

Former Postal Savings Bank 070
 Hold utca 4
Former Trade Union Headquarters 078
 Dózsa György út 84a
Főzelékfaló 062
 Hercegprímás utca
 T 266 3193

G

Gellért Bath 089
 Kelenhegyi út 4-6
 T 466 6166
 www.spasbudapest.com
Geppetto 081
 Katona József utca 15
 T 270 0107
 www.geppetto.hu
Gerbeaud 040
 Vörösmarty tér 7
 T 429 9020
 www.gerbeaud.hu
Goa 051
 Andrássy út 8
 T 302 2570
 www.goaworld.hu
Gresham Palace 038
 Roosevelt tér 5-6
 T 268 6000
 www.fourseasons.com

Gundel 048
Állatkerti utca 2
T 468 4040
www.gundel.hu

H
Honvéd Fencing Club 090
Dózsa György utca 55
Hotel Korona 096
Tündérpart 5
Eger
T 36 313 670
www.koronahotel.hu
Hotel Senator-Ház 096
Dobó-Platz 11
Eger
T 36 320 466
www.senatorhaz.hu
House of Terror 034
Andrássy út 60
T 374 2600
www.terrorhaza.hu
Hungarian Fencing Federation 090
Dózsa György utca 1-3
T 252 2149
Hungarian National Gallery 037
Buildings A-D
Buda Palace
Szent György tér 2
T 204 397 325
www.mng.hu

I
ING building 010
Dózsa György út 84b

L
Leroy Café 036
Ráday utca 11-13
T 219 5451
www.leroy.hu

M
Mai Manó Café 033
Nagymező utca 20
T 473 2666
www.maimano.hu
Menza 042
Liszt Ferenc tér 2
T 413 1482
www.menza.co.hu
Merlin 050
Gerlóczy utca 4
T 317 9338
www.merlinbudapest.org
Ministry of Transport and Postal Services 066
Dob utca 47
Modern and Breitner building 012
Deák Ferenc utca 11-13
Mokka 052
Sas utca 4
T 328 0081
www.mokkarestaurant.hu
Moszkva tér metro station 014
Moszkva tér
www.bkv.hu

N
Negro 055
Szent István tér 11
T 302 0391
New Theatre 065
Paulay Ede utca 35
T 269 6021
www.ujszinhaz.hu

New York Café 056
Erzsébet körút 9-11
T 886 6111
www.newyorkpalace.hu
Nosztalgia 082
Klauzál utca 1
T 322 8848
Nyugati Station 074
Nyugati tér
T 392 3800

P
The Palace of Arts 076
Komor Marcell utca 1
T 555 3001
www.mupa.hu
Palatinus Lido 069
Margitsziget
T 340 4505
Puskás Ferenc Stadion 072
Istvánmezei út 3-5
T 471 4100

R
Ráday Galeria 036
Ráday utca 28
T 217 6321
Retrock 087
Ferenczy István utca 28
T 0630 678 8430
www.retrock.com
Retrock Deluxe 087
Henszlmann Imre utca 1
T 0630 556 2814
www.retrock.com/deluxe.htm

Rudas Bath 089
Döbrentei tér 9
T 356 1322
www.spasbudapest.com

S
Spoon Café & Lounge 060
Pier 3
Vigadó tér
In front of Hotel InterContinental
T 411 0933
www.spooncafe.hu
Statue Park 100
Balatoni út/Szabadkai utca
T 424 7500
www.szoborpark.hu
Studio Agram 085
Falk Miksa utca 10
T 428 0653
www.studioagram.com
Szimpla Kert 046
Kazinczy utca 14
T 352 4198
www.szimpla.hu

T
Tisza Cipö 086
Károly körút 1
T 266 3055
www.tiszacipo.hu
Tom George 045
Október 6 utca 8
T 266 3525
Trafó Bár Tangó 062
Liliom utca 41
T 215 1600
Transformer Station 068
Dob utca 10

Tranzit Art Café 041
  Kosztolányi Dezső tér
  T 209 3070
  www.tranzitartcafe.hu

W
West-Balkán 040
  Kisfaludy utca 36
  T 371 1807
  www.west-balkan.com

Z
Zwack museum 084
  Soroksári út 26
  Entrance on Dandár utca 1
  T 476 2383
  www.zwack.hu

HOTELS
ADDRESSES AND ROOM RATES

Andrássy Hotel 020
Room rates:
double, €179;
Superior Room, €199
Andrássy út 111
T 462 2100
www.andrassyhotel.com

Art'otel 026
Room rates:
double, €120;
Superior Room, €150
Bem rakpart 16-19
T 487 9487
www.artotel.hu

Corinthia Grand Hotel Royal 016
Room rates:
double, €165
Erzsébet körút 43-49
T 479 4000
www.corinthiahotels.com

Danubius Hotel Gellért 016
Room rates:
double, €245
Szent Gellért tér 1
T 889 5500
www.danubiusgroup.com

Four Seasons Hotel
Gresham Palace 030
Room rates:
double, €245
Roosevelt tér 5-6
T 268 6000
www.fourseasons.com

Kempinksi Hotel Corvinus 028
Room rates:
double, €130;
Presidential Suite, €1,630
Erzsébet tér 7-8
T 429 3777
www.kempinski-budapest.com

Le Meridien 021
Room rates:
double, €140;
Deluxe Room, €270
Erzsébet tér 9-10
T 429 5500
www.lemeridien.com

New York Palace 024
Room rates:
double, €200;
Royal Suite, €4,000
Erzsébet körút 9-11
T 886 6111
www.newyorkpalace.hu

Parlament 017
Room rates:
Standard Double, €150
Kálmán Imre utca 19
T 374 6000
www.bestwestern.com

WALLPAPER* CITY GUIDES

Editorial Director
Richard Cook

Art Director
Loran Stosskopf
City Editor
Paul McCann
Editor
Rachael Moloney
Executive
Managing Editor
Jessica Firmin
Travel Bookings Editor
Sara Henrichs

Chief Designer
Benjamin Blossom
Designer
Daniel Shrimpton
Map Illustrator
Russell Bell
Photography Editor
Christopher Lands
Photography Assistant
Robin Key

Chief Sub-Editor
Jeremy Case
Sub-Editors
Catriona Luke
Stephen Patience
Assistant Sub-Editor
Milly Nolan
Interns
Tracy Fitzgerald
Chloe Godsell
Jemima Hills

Wallpaper* Group
Editor-in-Chief
Tony Chambers
Publishing Director
Andrew Black
Publisher
Neil Sumner

Contributors
Meirion Pritchard
Ellie Stathaki

Wallpaper* ® is a
registered trademark
of IPC Media Limited

All prices are correct at
time of going to press,
but are subject to change.

PHAIDON

Phaidon Press Limited
Regent's Wharf
All Saints Street
London N1 9PA

Phaidon Press Inc
180 Varick Street
New York, NY 10014

Phaidon® is a registered
trademark of Phaidon
Press Limited

www.phaidon.com

First published 2007
© 2007 IPC Media Limited

ISBN 978 0 7148 4737 5

A CIP Catalogue record for
this book is available from
the British Library.

Printed in China

PHOTOGRAPHERS

Paul Almasy/Corbis
Visegrád, pp102-103

Benjamin Blossom
Budapest city view,
inside front cover
Moszkva tér metro station,
pp014-015
House of Terror,
pp034-035
Former Postal Savings
Bank, pp070-071
Nyugati Station,
pp074-075
The Palace of Arts,
pp076-077

Alexis Chabala
Tisza Cipö, p086

Danita Delimont/Alamy
Eger, p097
Statue Park, pp100-101

Flashback Photo
Tranzit Art Café, p041
Merlin, p050
Goa, p051
Transformer Station, p068

Alexandre Guirkinger
ING building, pp010-011
Modern and Breitner
building, pp012-013

Parlament, p017,
pp018-019
Andrássy Hotel, p020
Le Meridien, p021,
pp022-023
New York Palace,
p024, p025
Kempinski Hotel Corvinus,
p028, p029
Mai Manó Café, p033
Leroy Café, p036
Castle District, p037
Gresham Palace,
pp038-039
Menza, pp042-043
Tom George, p045
Szimpla Kert, pp046-047
Gundel, pp048-049
Mokka, pp052-053
Dokk, p054
Negro, p055
New York Café, p056
A38, p057, pp058-059
New Theatre, p065
Ministry of Transport
and Postal Services,
pp066-067
Palatinus Lido, p069
Puskás Ferenc Stadion,
p072, p073
Former Trade Union
Headquarters, pp078-079
Geppetto, p081
Nosztalgia, pp082-083
Studio Agram, p085
Retrock Deluxe, p087

Rudas Bath, p089
Honvéd Fencing Club,
pp090-091
Alfred Hajós Sports
Swimming Pool, pp092-093
Danubius Health Spa Resort,
pp094-095

Patrice Hannicotte
Four Seasons Hotel Gresham
Palace, pp030-031

Mediacolors/Alamy
Esztergom, pp098-099

Marton Perlaki
Zsuzsa Kárpáti, p063

BUDAPEST
A COLOUR-CODED GUIDE TO THE HOT 'HOODS

FERENCVÁROS
The draw used to be the football – now it's rows of bars, boutiques and open-air clubs

TERÉZVÁROS
The city's most European district is all interiors stores, café culture, restaurants and wi-fi

ERZSÉBETVÁROS
This rapidly gentrifying boho Jewish quarter now has chic eateries and design centres

MARGITSZIGET
Recreation is writ large on this Danube island with pools, a classy spa and beer gardens

LIPÓTVÁROS AND BELVÁROS
Downtown is a treat of architectural styles, plus pleasant squares and historic cafés

VÁRHEGY, VÍZIVÁROS AND TABÁN
On the Danube's west bank are castles, palaces, Gothic churches, spas and design hotels

For a full description of each neighbourhood, see the Introduction.
Featured venues are colour-coded, according to the district in which they are located.